30 Days

To Overcome A

Shitty Job

A Mindfulness Program with a Touch of Humor

Corin Devaso

Copyright © JV 2021

Share your journey!

Let people know you're practicing mindfulness! Post a picture of the cover and include #30DaysNow via social media. Our various guides share the same lessons, so you can see how others are using mindfulness on their journey!

Don't forget that each exercise has a unique hashtag for online sharing.

This book is meant to be a guide only, and does not guarantee specific results. If the lessons and exercises in this book are followed, change can occur for certain people. Results vary from person to person; some people may not need to complete the thirty days to experience change, but it's encouraged that the entire program be read completely through at least once.

The last half of the book consists of blank note pages that the reader can use in conjunction with the exercises for each day. The reader is encouraged to utilize the note pages; though it's not necessary.

Give the gift of mindfulness. See similar guides at www.30DaysNow.com if you wish to purchase a book for a loved one. **See the disclosure below.**

Disclosure (Shared Lessons and Exercises):
Keep in mind that our mindfulness guides share the same lessons and exercises, so there is no need to purchase more than one book; unless you are sharing with a group or giving the guides as gifts. Our mindfulness guides are created for various topics; however, they utilize the same lessons and exercises, so please be aware of this before purchasing. For example, *30 Days to Overcome a Shitty Job* will mostly have the same lessons and exercises as *30 Days to Reduce Stress* and so forth. By reading just one of our guides, you'll be able to apply the same lessons and exercises to multiple areas of your life.

Enjoy your journey of self-discovery!

Contents

Preface..4

Day 1..8
Day 2..9
Day 3..10
Day 4..11
Day 5..12
Day 6..13
Day 7..14
Day 8..15
Day 9..16
Day 10..17
Day 11..18
Day 12..19
Day 13..20
Day 14..21
Day 15..22
Day 16..23
Day 17..24
Day 18..25
Day 19..26
Day 20..27
Day 21..28
Day 22..29
Day 23..30
Day 24..31
Day 25..32
Day 26..33
Day 27..34
Day 28..35
Day 29..36
Day 30..37

Conclusion..38
Note Pages...Begins on 39

Preface

If you have been stuck in a job that's crushing your soul, hindering your growth, repressing your confidence, and making you feel like the most depressed employee on the planet, then this 30 day mindfulness program will be of immense help. It is time to break free from the ways of thinking that have kept you enslaved to a miserable job.

You are not alone in this common dilemma - many people experience the same thoughts and feelings regarding their shitty jobs; but few take the time and effort to mindfully gain awareness and live free of debilitating work. You can be one of the few who takes the courage to look at the problem with a clear mind and heart.

Let's define *shitty job*: A shitty job is essentially any job that you do out of pure desperation, confusion, basic need, or unawareness. It may even be for a mix of these reasons. The job leaves you feeling drained of spirit, soul, and heart. A shitty job is any job that leaves you feeling deeply unfulfilled. Simply put, a shitty job is any job that makes you feel like shit.

Most people obtain and keep shitty jobs for basic needs first and foremost – to earn money to pay bills, buy food, have shelter, establish health insurance, and to accumulate savings for education and retirement. Even when these basic needs are well met, most people continue with their shitty jobs because of deeply enmeshed thought patterns that hold no weight in reality, but appear to. Absurd as it may seem, many people in shitty jobs have their basic needs met, or have the means necessary to meet those needs, yet stay ensnared by the dependency.

It's as if holding onto a shitty job has become honorable, meritorious, and admirable. In truth, keeping a shitty job is flat out crazy. But don't feel discouraged if you are stuck in the grips of one, because as mentioned, you're not alone and this is a very common predicament. Look around you on your way to work - the people you see on the highway, in the train car, or on the bus are usually headed to jobs that they consider shitty. If they were going somewhere meaningful and fulfilling, they'd look a lot happier. That's not to say that all people are unhappy with their jobs, but the majority are. After this program, you won't be one of them.

The following pages involve a 30 day program made up of lessons and exercises to help you overcome ways of thinking, feelings, and habits that have kept you stuck in a shitty job. Though these lessons and exercises can be applied to any unhealthy reliance, this program will focus specifically on the problem of keeping a job that is draining your life of energy.

For some readers, they'll overcome the reliance quickly and will drop their unhealthy thoughts and habits in no time; and for others, they'll overcome slowly and gradually. In either case, if you stick with the program you'll start to witness your shitty job's grip weaken. Please don't judge your progress in the program, as this isn't a competition and there isn't a goal you must attain. Let the debilitating thoughts, feelings, habits, and dependency simply drop as you work through the exercises and lessons.

It's not necessary to complete the days in order, nor should you be religious about completing them successfully. There is no such thing as a successful completion of this program. The bottom line is to observe and awaken, and that cannot be obtained through success, force, pressure, struggle, or competition. Simply relax, follow the program, and the grip of the job will loosen.

You'll also notice that mindfulness, silence, and stillness are a regular discipline for each day in the program. Because you've been influenced by a dependency based society that demands instant gratification, silence and stillness may seem nearly impossible for you to practice. For this reason, we'll incorporate this discipline from the outset. A quiet and still mind is an incredibly powerful resource, but one that requires daily maintenance.

It should also be noted that you're not required to quit your job, think about leaving your job, or get fired. The point being: by practicing the following exercises and lessons in the days to come, you won't even need willpower to drop the shitty job – it'll just happen.

One of the most important lessons to keep in mind is to not fight the constraint of the shitty job while participating in this program. Dependencies, habits, and strong patterns of thinking are empowered by a fight and struggle. Keep your shitty job for the length of this program without regret or remorse; unless you have an opportunity to leave. Shitty jobs, like most tools of an imperfect society, feed on negative thought patterns, fear, and struggle. This program will help you overcome without conflict.

You'll need about 15-30 minutes per day for the program; but feel free to spend more time if needed. The amount of time doesn't matter, as long as you're in an environment that allows you to concentrate without distraction. Also to be mentioned, the last portion of this book includes note pages that you can use with the exercises. It's encouraged that you write down any thoughts, insights, adaptations, lessons, mantras, etc, on those blank pages. The note pages can also be used to rip out and take with you. Feel free to use them as you wish.

One last thing: If you're like most people, you might be dependent on caffeine, alcohol, or sugar to some extent. If you are, do your best to lessen the consumption of these substances over the next 30 days. It's not necessary that you abstain, but can you cut consumption of these substances in half, or more? It's important that your mind is sober and your body relaxed to make the most of these exercises and lessons.

Let's get started.

Let others know you're practicing mindfulness! Post a picture of the cover and include #30DaysNow. Also, don't forget that each exercise has a unique hashtag for online sharing.

Share your journey and discover other people practicing mindfulness!

Day 1
(Share this experience using #30DaysBreathing)
Exercise:

Find a place without distraction, and turn off all electronics. Sit with your back straight, kneel, or lie on a hard surface (not bed) and remain in silence for 10 minutes.

During these 10 minutes, take deep and focused breaths and hold them for a few seconds each. Exhale slowly. Listen intently to your breathing. Don't try to change it – simply listen, and feel the air go in and out.

*When you're ready, repeat the mantra: "**Be still. Be silent.**" Repeat this slowly multiple times out loud as well as quietly. You might experience boredom or anxiety, but continue repeating the mantra regardless. Repeat it until you're calm and ready. You can continue the deep breathing during the mantra, or take deep breaths during pauses. Don't rush.*

Each of the 30 days will have this time of silence, focused breathing, and a mantra. Except this page, the end of each day's page will remind you of the minutes you are to spend in silence and focused breathing for the day; and will also have a mantra for you to practice. You can repeat the mantras during your times of silence and focused breathing, or following. Remember, there is no right or wrong way to do this.

If you're going to your shitty job today, practice the focused breathing and mantra while there. Negativity wants to fight; in fact, it's energized by fighting. Instead of fighting the shitty job with adverse emotion, meet it with focused breathing, silence, and observation.

Day 2
(Share this experience using #30DaysPonder)

Exercise:

Ponder this question: Can you remember a time in your life when you didn't feel constrained by a shitty job?

Writing is extremely beneficial to the mind; especially when pondering. Write down your thoughts about this particular question. If your mind drifts, then write whatever thoughts emerge. It's okay if you have nothing to write, but ponder the question regardless.

Were you able to remember a period in your life when you were happy at work? If you're like many people in western civilization, you may have to return to old memories to determine that period. It's not uncommon for a person to be stuck in a shitty job for a long time, developing an unhealthy dependency on it. After a while, a person in a shitty job forgets what fulfilling work actually feels like.

Recognize that your dependency on the shitty job has deep roots; it's been growing for a while. However, the dependency can be dropped quickly and completely; and you have the capability to overcome it.

*10 minutes of silence and focused breathing. Repeat the mantra: **"Drop. Unlearn. Discover."**

Day 3
(Share this experience using #30DaysDoorway)

Exercise:

Stand in front of a doorway, with the door open. Close your eyes, and take a deep breath. With eyes closed and holding your breath, step through the doorway. Once you have stepped through completely, open your eyes and exhale.

Doorways are amazing tools that can be used for practicing mindfulness and observation. How often do you rush through doors without paying attention to the change of environment? We don't often pay attention or appreciate the transition; we simply rush through unaware that our perspective has changed. This isn't a bad thing; in fact, it's great that we don't stall in front of doorways, too afraid to enter the next environment. At the beginning of this exercise you were in a particular place, and then you stepped through a doorway into a completely different setting. You made a transition without worry or concern, and very naturally.

When it comes to physical doorways, we rarely stop and worry about the change of environment – we just walk through and accept the new experience. You can apply this same lesson to decisions regarding your shitty job, such as if you should stay or leave. Step through the decision and accept the change, whatever you decide; but try to step through aware of the transition and grateful for the experience. There will always be doorways to step through.

*10 minutes of silence and focused breathing. Repeat the mantra: **"I accept change with awareness and gratitude."**

Day 4
(Share this experience using #30DaysBody)

Exercise:

Observe your body. Observe how it feels, moves, and reacts. More direction is explained below.

While at your shitty job, observe your body movements, sounds, sensations, and breaths throughout the day. Do you take long and deep breaths, or short and hurried breaths? Do you sit most of the day; if so, how do you sit? How often do you blink? How much do you walk and lift? What's the tone of your voice when you speak with people? Are you relaxed, or tense? Try to observe everything about your body while at work. Be aware of its movements and sensations. Be aware of how the shitty job is affecting your body, either positively or negatively.

If you are not at the shitty job today, then continue with the 10 minutes of silence and focused breathing, but get in touch with your body. A good way to do this is by touching each body part and saying its name, leaving your hand on the part for a few seconds and feeling its texture and warmth. Start with your head: place your hand on your head and say, "*I am touching my head.*" And then work your way down to your shoulders, arms, stomach, legs, knees, and feet. Focus your attention on one body part at a time. Say its name and describe what you are touching.

*10 minutes of silence and focused breathing. Repeat the mantra: "*I am not my body.*"

Day 5
(Share this experience using #30DaysIdentity)

Exercise:

On a piece of paper, write down all the labels and adjectives that you and others use to identify you.

For example, do you see yourself as a son, daughter, mother, father, student, teacher, cashier, friend, engineer, accountant, employee, employer, roommate, husband, wife, etc? And what adjectives do you use to label yourself; for example, do you identify yourself as failed, successful, happy, depressed, good, moral, unethical, lustful, greedy, valuable, worthless, etc? Don't only write down the labels and descriptions you perceive; but also write down what you believe others label you as: do you believe others see you as a valuable friend, stupid and incompetent employee, extremely smart and talented worker, etc? Take as long as you need, and fill up a sheet of paper with those labels and descriptions.

After you've done that, tear the paper into multiple pieces and throw it away. Those labels and adjectives mean nothing. They're not "you." You cannot be defined, labeled, described, or controlled by titles, positive or negative. Most people poison their conscience with such learned vocabulary. They really believe these words hold power – they'll even fight, stress out, become ill, and die to make these words part of reality. Shitty jobs, as well as most devices of society, teach you to identify with particular words, which are only thoughts. Unlearn them.

*10 minutes of silence and focused breathing. Repeat the mantra: "**I am not a label, title, or description.**

Day 6
(Share this experience using #30DaysCount)

Exercise:

Count to 25 slowly, pausing for a few seconds before the next number; then, count backward from 25 slowly. Try this with your eyes closed. While counting up you can imagine yourself being lifted into the sky; and then while counting down, descending back to earth.

Our world today is about speed. Everyone seems to be in a rush, yet most of them are unsatisfied; and, they have no clue where they're going. Chasing the next best thing is a fruitless endeavor. It's the rare person who slows down to enjoy the present moment, regardless of its nature. Because there seems to be so many problems, and most jobs are focused on resolving those problems, people are compelled to accept anxiety and rush toward a reward and conclusion. That surely isn't happiness. Happiness can only be found in the present moment, not in a hypothetical future of rewards and successes. Rushing is another form of going nowhere.

How many times have you rushed through tasks at your shitty job? This is destructive to your peace of mind and health: concentration suffers, stress levels rise, and awareness to the present moment isn't possible.

It's critical to slow down. You only have one life to live – don't rush through it, and don't be dependent on anything that encourages you to rush. Be still, and slow down.

*10 minutes of silence and focused breathing. Repeat the mantra: **"Slow down. Do not rush. Enjoy the present moment."**

Day 7
(Share this experience using #30DaysGrip)

Exercise:

Find a hard object that you can hold in the palm of your hand (such as a stone, ball, or bottle). With either hand, grip this object tightly and squeeze it as hard as you can. Squeeze it forcefully until you can't hold on to it any longer. Drop the object when ready.

If you could continue squeezing that object forever, perhaps you would; but your muscles and nerves can only endure for so long. At some point, you simply and quickly release the grip and drop the object. There isn't a process to the drop; it just happens when your body says that's enough. The release happens naturally without effort.

Letting go of an unhealthy dependency, habit, thought pattern, addiction, emotion, or behavior can be that easy. Letting go can be as natural and guilt free as dropping the object you were gripping on to so tightly in this exercise; so, take a lesson from your body's experience. When it's time to let go, then let go. The time to let go is always now. Just let the drop happen.

If you believe this lesson is telling you to quit your shitty job immediately, then you're missing the point; however, if that's what you perceived, then perhaps you should leave it. The point is: whatever you are gripping so tightly, just release it – let it go, naturally and without effort.

*10 minutes of silence and focused breathing. Repeat the mantra: **"Letting go is natural. I can let go, here and now."**

Day 8
(Share this experience using #30DaysSketch)

Exercise:

One a piece of paper (large enough to draw on), quickly draw a sketch of your environment: the bedroom, office, park, kitchen, airplane, building, town, bus, etc...that you are in. You don't need to be a skilled artist, just draw an outline of the environment using lines and boxes.

Don't spend more than 5 minutes on this drawing. It is best if you draw an environment that you are in daily, such as your shitty job, but any environment will do. After you're done, you can keep or throw away the paper – as you wish.

Most of us are in the same environment day in, day out. We're in the same home, workplace, city, car, stores, and buildings for a long time, sometimes years; and for some people, life. This isn't a bad thing; however, we have an interesting way of associating ourselves with our environment. We begin to believe that it's a part of us; when in fact it's simply an environment. Too many people allow their surroundings to define their essential selves.

A great way of seeing yourself apart from your daily surroundings is to observe your environment. Drawing your surroundings allows you to slow down, be still, and look at your environment from a new perspective. Realize that you are not the environment of your shitty job, regardless of how long you've been there. Wake up and see that it doesn't define you.

*10 minutes of silence and focused breathing. Repeat the mantra: *"I am not the environment I experience."*

Day 9
(Share this experience using #30DaysCoin)

Exercise:

Find a coin. While standing, flip the coin and let it land wherever. If it lands with the head side up, spin around to the right until you come back to your original place; if it lands tail side up, spin around to the left until you come back to your original place. Again, head side up, spin to the right; tail side up, spin to the left – doing a full circle until you return to your original standing position.

In which direction did you spin? In this exercise, you left the direction of your movement completely up to the flip, the coin, and gravity. When you spun, you experienced a specific visual perception of the environment that you would not have had from spinning in the opposite direction. But, you returned to the same position regardless. The experience would have been different if you spun to the opposite side; and if you repeat this exercise multiple times, your experiences in the same direction will be different as well. The point being: it doesn't matter what direction you go in or what you experience; you'll always return to the present moment.

People in shitty jobs ruminate about *what ifs* and *shoulds*: *"What if I stay at this shitty job forever?" "Should I leave this shitty job today, or stick it out for another year?" "If I quit, will I be fine? What if I don't find a better job?"* Those thoughts just spin and spin, strengthening the reliance with fear and worry. The direction you take doesn't matter; because you'll always return to the present.

*10 minutes of silence and focused breathing. Repeat the mantra: *"**The direction does not matter. I am present.**"*

Day 10
(Share this experience using #30DaysLies)

Exercise:

On a sheet of paper (any size) write down all the internal lies that you regularly hear about yourself – i.e. within your mind. Focus specifically on the lies about your shitty job.

Now, tear the paper into multiple pieces, and throw away.

It's common to have an internal voice (or voices) within your mind, playing a record of lies over and over. We eventually begin to accept these lies and let them impact our growth and happiness. Most people you see on a daily basis have these recurring internal voices; and most people are oblivious to them – sort of like white noise. This isn't a mental illness, but a way in which the mind works. We all experience these internal quiet voices whispering untruths about our being. These lies are nothing to fear, but need to be observed. Writing them down helps you observe and become aware of their deceptions.

The power of the silence, focused breathing, and mantras, which you have been practicing, is to draw out the lies. Let them manifest, and observe them. Common internal lies about shitty jobs include: *"You are a loser; you'll always have a shitty job" "You have become nothing, and you will never improve," "You are worthless. No one else will hire you" "You'll always be job searching"* and so on. These thoughts are not part of you; however, the deception is to make you believe they are. Like many things in society, shitty jobs and employers clandestinely plant such lies.

*10 minutes of silence and focused breathing. Repeat the mantra: **"Thoughts are only thoughts - nothing more."**

Day 11
(Share this experience using #30DaysBlue)

Exercise:

Today, look for the color blue in your surrounding environment. If possible, spend the entire day looking for the color blue in the places you go. Whether you're doing this exercise in a bedroom, office, classroom, outside, or at your shitty job, look for the color blue in all things that surround you. If you think you'll forget to do this throughout the entire day, spend at least 20 focused minutes practicing this exercise at some point.

Focused attention is something that must be practiced - it doesn't come easy in our rapid paced society. Instead of encouraging us to focus and observe, the modern world encourages us to rush and get things done.

Searching for a color or shape helps to slow down our accelerated and cyclical thought patterns, and reminds us that there's more to the world than the chaotic thoughts we collectively and daily experience. By searching for the color blue, your mind can escape the fictitious grip of anxiety, lust, desire, depression, worry, fear, or any other potent emotion. When you are at your shitty job, are you aware of the colors around you? Most likely not.

Negative perceptions of your shitty job distract your conscience from reality. Look for the color blue today, and wake up to life in the present moment, even at your shitty job. Whether you have the shittiest job or the greatest job on the planet, you can always enjoy the present.

*10 minutes of silence and focused breathing. Repeat the mantra: *"I am focused, here and now."*

Day 12
(Share this experience using #30DaysHobby)

Exercise:

On a sheet of paper (one that you can easily save and return to later) make a list of hobbies that you've had in the past but have neglected, and also make a list of hobbies that you would like to start in the future.

From these lists choose one hobby from the past and one new hobby that you'd like to start. Focus only on these two – the old hobby and the new one. Make this a priority.

How often have you said, or have heard other people say, *"I wish I had the time."* You do have the time, even with a shitty job. You just choose to think of time in the way that you've been taught to perceive it. If your life depended on it, you would certainly make the time if needed.

In fact, time is a manmade construct - don't ever forget that. There is only the present moment. Past and future are not here and now. We spend far too much time thinking about time. How many of your recurrent inner thoughts involve questions such as, *"When will that ever happen?" "When will I ever change?" "Why did that have to happen?" "If the past were different, life would be better."* These are lies that only eat into the present moment, and infect our modern world.

Adverse feelings and thoughts about your shitty job occupy the present moment, which could be used to pursue hobbies and other things that magnify your happiness.

*10 minutes of silence and focused breathing. Repeat the mantra: *"**The time is now. Happiness is present.**"*

Day 13
(Share this experience using #30DaysGSR)

Exercise:

Say the words "Guilt", "Shame", and "Regret" 10 times to yourself out loud. Don't rush. Pause between each repetition. For the pause, you can take a deep breath. Your eyes can remain open or closed. Again, don't rush - say the words slowly and observe any thoughts, feelings, or images that emerge internally.

Now, say these words again 10 times, but with a smile.

What futile credence we give words such as Guilt, Shame and Regret. We use these words on ourselves as well as others; they become regular vocabulary for our internal recurring voices. And in the end, they're mere words that hold no power. What would these words be without a facial expression, tone, inflection, or emphasis?

When you said these three specific words, what thoughts came to mind, what did you feel, and was there a reaction in your body? If there is a reaction, such as shortness of breath or a frown, people tend to interpret it as sadness; but this reaction is a learned behavior. We've been taught to feel and think a certain way with regard to guilt, shame, and regret. The truth is: these words mean nothing.

Shitty jobs, like many societal tools, flourish on these three words and the learned reactions they produce. But see them for what they are…mere words with no power.

*10 minutes of silence and focused breathing. Repeat the mantra: **"I am not Guilt. I am not Shame. I am not Regret."**

Day 14
(Share this experience using #30DaysBreak)

Exercise:

Find an object that you can break: an egg, a drinking glass, a pencil...anything. In a safe place, break the object of your choice, and be especially careful if it's glass or something sharp. Don't clean up the pieces or mess immediately, observe it and let the pieces sit for at least a few minutes.

Did you break the object, or did I break the object by asking you to break it? And if you believe it was solely you who broke the object, did the object allow you to break it? This isn't an exercise meant to release frustration or stress. The purpose of this lesson is to show you that you're not 100% responsible for the perceived chaos, mess, loss, or broken pieces caused by your shitty job.

Destruction happens in the present moment, and that's OK. We spend so much time worrying about goals, relationships, jobs, situations, the future, and other things breaking into pieces. And when that happens, we tend to blame ourselves or others, because that's what we've been taught to do. Allow breaking to happen; and observe the pieces.

You might feel that a shitty job has broken you, or is about to break you. Let it happen; don't fight it. Whatever the breaking, pieces, and mess look like; just observe what occurs. You cannot break the present moment. You'll be OK.

*10 minutes of silence and focused breathing. Repeat the mantra: "***I cannot harm or break the present moment.***"

Day 15

(Share this experience using #30DaysBathroom)

Exercise:

This exercise may seem frivolous, but give it a try; because it may be one of the lessons that benefits you most.

For the remainder of the day, whenever you use the bathroom, for any reason, take your time with what you're doing. Don't rush through the process, like you may normally do. Focus on taking your time in the bathroom; do every step of your bathroom experience twice as slow. It may even help to say each step: "I am now sitting up straight on the toilet," "I am now putting soap on my hands," "I am now drying my hands," etc.

Most people hurry up their bathroom experience, not realizing what they're doing – forcing, not standing or sitting straight, not relaxing, not washing their hands properly, not drying their hands slowly. They rush in and out, like they have somewhere important to go. Don't be like that any longer. Take your time in the bathroom; it's not only unhealthy for the body to rush the excretion process, but it's also unhealthy for the mind. A rushed bathroom experience doesn't allow you to live in the present moment. Allow the excretion and cleaning to happen naturally with a relaxed and focused attention.

This is also a great exercise to practice every day at your shitty job, as long as you're still working there. Slowing down will allow you to think clearly and perceive the shitty job as well as new opportunities in a fresh way.

*10 minutes of silence and focused breathing. Repeat the mantra: **"Don't hurry. Stay present. Stay still."**

Day 16
(Share this experience using #30DaysSmile)

Exercise:

Hold a smile for 5 minutes. You don't need to do this exercise in front of a mirror; but feel free to do so if you wish. You can even do this exercise during the 15 minutes of silence and focused breathing today. While holding your smile, take a moment and feel your face; actually touch the smile and the curvature of your lips and cheek bones.

Have you ever behaved a certain way and then saw your mood change immediately? Physical exercise, such as running and weightlifting, does this for many people. Certain forms of yoga have also been used by people to change their moods. The point is: changing your behavior not only impacts other people, but can also impact your perception of yourself.

You'll notice that while you're smiling during this exercise, you may experience certain emotions. You might feel silly, embarrassed, stupid, funny, weird, or whatever. Continue smiling regardless. In fact, if you are still struggling with a shitty job at this point in the program, smile while you're there – simply practice smiling throughout the work day; set a reminder alarm if needed. As always, observe your thoughts while you're smiling; observe the thoughts as if they're clouds passing by in a bright blue sky.

Smiling causes an authentic reaction in our bodies and minds that is essentially good. The present moment enjoys a nice smile. So hold that smile until you no longer can.

*15 minutes of silence and focused breathing. Repeat the mantra: **"Happiness is now. I am happy."**

Day 17
(Share this experience using #30DaysScribble)

Exercise:

Take a piece of paper (any size, but large enough to draw on); with a pen, scribble a random line with your eyes closed. Don't lift your pen from the paper; keep it as one messy scribble. Only spend two or three seconds doing this.

Now, with your eyes open and seeing what your scribble looks like, make it into an actual image of something. Work with the scribble to make something noticeable.

What did you make out of your scribble: an animal, house, drifting balloon, kite, a person, a scenario, an entire scene with many things, etc?

This is one of my favorite exercises. It's a lesson that teaches that the scribbles and confusions we experience in life can be changed and formed with a new perspective. Life is all about perspective. How do you perceive scribble, mess, chaos, clutter, disarray, and confusion in your life experience? Do you know that you can perceive it differently starting now?

In silence, stillness, and with an open mind, take a look at any scribbles that you may be experiencing in life, especially with regard to your shitty job. If you observe long enough, without judgment or concern, you will gain a new perspective. Imagine your shitty job as the scribble on your piece of paper; what can you see differently?

*15 minutes of silence and focused breathing. Repeat the mantra: **"Perception can change in the present moment."**

Day 18

(Share this experience using #30DaysTrash)

Exercise:

Go out and buy a small trash can. You should be able to find one cheaply. If you don't have the funds for this exercise, you can use an empty box or container; however, a small trash can works better for its symbolism.

Designate this specific trash can your "concerns and worries can" (or use any title you wish) – some people benefit from writing this label directly onto the can.

Now, write down (on scraps of paper or whatever paper you wish to use) any concerns, worries, and adverse thoughts that you may be experiencing today, and throw them into the can. Try to practice this every day: quickly write down worries, concerns, and negative thoughts, and then throw them into the can. It may be beneficial to have a supply of scrap paper near the can for easy access.

This exercise may seem simple, but let's go beyond throwing your written concerns, worries, and thoughts away. Designate a few times during the week for sifting through the can and taking out random worries and concerns from days prior – just reach in and pull some out. Observe them, but don't judge yourself. This is a great exercise to learn your negative thought patterns and the lies that grip your conscience. If you stick with this practice, you may gain a deeper understanding into the dependencies, habits, thought patterns, and feelings that have you stuck by a shitty job.

*15 minutes of silence and focused breathing. Repeat the mantra: **"There is nothing to worry about. All is well."**

Day 19
(Share this experience using #30DaysPatience)

Exercise:

Listen to a person intently without interruption. Only speak if the person asks you a question, but don't give a long answer. Make the conversation entirely theirs. Give them the floor, and listen to every word they are saying. Again, do not interrupt. Observe their words and facial expressions without judgment. Be patient and relaxed, even if they speak for more than a few minutes.

Patience is a dying practice in our digital age. It appears that all business involves the perceived need to go faster, faster, and faster. Quicker responses, faster uploads, more data, rapid analysis, accelerated transportation, and all sorts of chop-chop. This false need for speed has seeped deep into our collective psyche. The western world is filled with anxiously demanding people, going nowhere fast.

This widespread lack of patience has caused a problem with regard to listening to one another. It has also caused dependency on shitty jobs to manifest; because employees are not patient enough to neither build meaningful relationships nor listen carefully for new opportunities.

Practicing patience by listening intently to someone speak is a great way to slow down the mind and build meaningful relationships. The fabricated relationship between you and your shitty job cannot compete with real human interaction, which requires patience. Practice patience at work.

*15 minutes of silence and focused breathing. Repeat the mantra: *"Listen. Be patient. Listen."*

Day 20
(Share this experience using #30DaysBalance)

Exercise:

If you can stand, stand on one foot and try to stay balanced as long as possible. If you're unable to stand, balance a pen on your wrist or index finger, trying not to let it fall.

Now, let your elevated foot, or the balanced pen, drop. Don't force the drop, just let it happen naturally.

All abnormal dependencies want you to balance them with necessary dependencies (eating, drinking, breathing, moving, sensing, etc). Your shitty job doesn't want you to consider it abnormal or damaging to your baseline happiness. It wants you to believe that you can keep it in balance with your basic needs for survival. This is an effective lie of the dependency; and in fact, all dependencies use this lie to keep you hooked.

Understand that your reliance on the shitty job doesn't help you at all; even in a balanced state. Let's say a person can balance a shitty job with their responsibilities to care for family, have fun, and stay healthy. The person is fooling themselves, and the shitty job is slowly but surely taking from present moment awareness. It would be better if this person let the balance fail and watch the shitty job drop to either side – that is, either completely impacting their lives negatively (many call this *rock bottom*) or letting it pass away, like a dark cloud passing in a blue sky.

If you've still been balancing this shitty job; let it drop.

*15 minutes of silence and focused breathing. Repeat the mantra: "**It is okay to let go. I can let go.**"

Day 21
(Share this experience using #30DaysSymbol)

Exercise:

Choose a physical symbol that will remind you to observe and be aware in the present moment. Try to choose something from nature, or that is made of natural material.

The object you choose can be anything, but it's best if it's something that you can enjoy looking at and touching. For example, many walkers and hikers will find a unique rock small enough to carry in their hands. A stone, necklace, bracelet, seashell, cedar block, coin…anything will do, as long as you enjoy it and you can dedicate it as a tool for remembrance.

Another cunning trick of a shitty job is to confuse the mind into forgetting you're part of the natural world. By having a symbol of remembrance, you can reconnect with the present moment. This symbol isn't meant to be an idol, god, or icon. Don't think too deeply into this. The symbol is simply a tool to help you remember where you are in the *here and now*. Shitty jobs have a keen way of impacting our understanding that we're wonderful beings in a natural world. As long as you're aware of the present moment, you'll have no desire to return to the lies, illusions, and hallucinations of a shitty job.

*15 minutes of silence and focused breathing. Repeat the mantra: **"All is well. Here and now, all is well."**

Day 22
(Share this experience using #30DaysWalk)

Exercise:

Go for a mindfulness walk for at least 10 minutes. Focus on each step. Feel the steps: the feel of your feet hitting the ground, your heel rolling forward, your toes, the bend of your knees, your hips working to balance your posture, the swinging of your arms, etc. Don't rush; go slow. Focus on your breathing as well. Get in tune with your body as you step. Pay attention to your physical senses throughout the walk. Focus – don't listen to music or be distracted.

Human beings have always used walking as a natural therapeutic exercise. There is something about walking, and focusing on the walk, that calms the mind and soul. The longer one walks, the more relaxed the person feels.

Any moment is a good time to walk and experience your inner and outer environment. During long walks, thoughts will emerge that will allow you to graciously observe them. Let the thoughts pass; you may even have emotions that emerge, observe those and let them pass as well. Focusing on your steps will help you clear the mind of clutter left over from a shitty job. Walking in the early morning and at dusk is especially beneficial.

A 20 minute walk brings more comfort, stillness, peace, focus, and awareness than thousands of hours at a shitty job. Walk every day, as much as you can. If you are able to walk at breaks during your shitty job, take the opportunity and go for a mindfulness walk.

*15 minutes of silence and focused breathing. Repeat the mantra: *"I am relaxed. I am at peace."*

Day 23

(Share this experience using #30DaysSway)

Exercise:

Stand still for 5 minutes; with knees slightly bent. At first try to remain still, but then let your body sway. Let it move any way it wishes. Feel its movement. If you're unable to stand, you can do this same exercise by extending your arm or leg from a sitting position – try to keep it straight, but then let go of trying and allow movement to happen.

We tend to lock ourselves into particular goals, expectations, thought patterns, and habits. We even go so far as to admire and honor rigidity – people mistake rigidity for perseverance. This is taught and told to us by our culture. Everything around you may be shouting, even in a quiet whisper, that you must remain submissive and obedient.

A shitty job, like most dependencies, is no different in its message. It wants you to remain rigid; not to be released from its hold. If you freely moved on from a shitty job, it would lose you as an employee, slave, and dependent. Who wants to remain rigidly dependent on something like a shitty job for happiness? Or I should say…false happiness.

The message of a shitty job essentially says, *"You need to work here. I own you. If you left, you would prove to be a lazy piece of shit. The right thing to do is to stay and obey."* Allow your body and mind to move on from the lie. Trust that your body and mind will sway to its own rhythm, and away from the shitty job.

*15 minutes of silence and focused breathing. Repeat the mantra: *"I am now free to move. I am free to move on."*

Day 24

(Share this experience using #30DaysWorstCase)

Exercise:

Think of a major worry that consistently upsets you about your shitty job. On a sheet of paper, write down three worst case scenarios for that dominating concern. For example, if someone is persistently worried about what may result from quitting a shitty job, that individual can write as a worst case scenario, "I will end up on the streets, living out of homeless shelters. I'll lose everything." As mentioned, write down three different worst case scenarios for your specific worry.

Now, next to each of those three worst case scenarios write, "If this happens, I accept this."

Worry is an illness that goes untreated in most people. Think of worry like a cancer of the spirit; but few people know how to treat it effectively. One of the only ways to eradicate worry isn't to fight, ignore, or run from it; but to face it in the present moment and accept it for the illusion it is. You can never be worried about something happening in the present moment – that's impossible; you can only be worried about the future, which is always illusory.

Writing down your worries and worst case scenarios, if they ever do come true (which they rarely do), is a great way to draw those thoughts out of your mind and into the present moment, allowing you to face, accept, and observe them.

*15 minutes of silence and focused breathing. Repeat the mantra: **"Worries are not real. They are passing thoughts."**

Day 25
(Share this experience using #30DaysName)

Exercise:

Choose a new first name. You can also use your middle name for this exercise.

Now, whenever you're in public this week, introduce yourself using your new name. For example, if you are ordering food or making reservations, use the new name. Whenever you're in a situation that doesn't require your original first name, use the new first name instead. Do this until you have used the new name at least three times.

If you introduced yourself to a stranger using the new name, you may have felt awkward or guilty – as if you weren't being truthful about your identity. Ponder this for a moment. Observe the feelings and thoughts that you experienced using the new name. Were you feeling dishonest? Do you still exist without your name?

We have become conditioned to attach our beings to the most lifeless things. Names are lifeless; they do not exist in reality. They are sounds that are produced; a combination of letters; however, we engrave them on tombstones as if they preserve the present being which inhabits the body. Names are not bad; they are necessary for particular legal means; but don't attach yourself to your name. From time to time, practice using a different name to remind yourself that you are not controlled by sounds and symbols.

*15 minutes of silence and focused breathing. Repeat the mantra: *"I am not a name, sound, or symbol."*

Day 26
(Share this experience using #30DaysLose)

Exercise:

Choose an object that you use and rely on every day, and that you sometimes lose – such as a key, cell phone, pen, hat, toothbrush, or television controller.

Now, actually attempt to lose this object. Hide it well, and try to make yourself forget where it is.

More than likely you won't be able to lose this object, as hard as you try, because you have applied a lot of attention to the process of losing it and trying to make yourself forget. At this point, losing it is nearly impossible. Why do you think this is?

If you try to drop a dependency, behavior, thought pattern, addiction, or any unhealthy vice using a lot of thought, attention, focus, struggle, and effort…you'll never lose it. It will be with you in one form or another for a very long time, possibly forever. The point is: whatever you give attention to consistently, will be difficult to lose. This is the reason why people who complain a lot are never happy – they can't stop giving thought and attention to the problems they're grumbling about. The problems eventually become an intimate part of their lives. If you continue giving thought and attention to the shittiness of your job, it'll always have a hold on your life. Remember, rival enemies maintain a devoted relationship. Don't be an enemy of your job.

*15 minutes of silence and focused breathing. Repeat the mantra: *"I am not my job. I am not thoughts of my job."*

Day 27
(Share this experience using #30DaysPinch)

Exercise:

Pinch the skin on the back of your hand or forearm until there is discomfort and slight pain. It's not necessary to pinch hard enough to bruise yourself, just enough to feel a small burn.

Did I cause the pain by asking you to do this exercise? No; you caused this pain to yourself – think about this carefully. You even decided how much pain to give yourself, and when to relieve the pain. You can't blame me or anyone else for the pain you just experienced. You were solely responsible. You were also responsible for letting go.

This is easily understood with regard to physical pain, such as pinching oneself; however, we have a lot of difficulty understanding this lesson as it applies to adverse emotions and feelings. How often have you said, and have heard others say, *"My job makes me so depressed", "I need to get out of my job; it's killing me", "I'm so frustrated that my boss sucks so much", or, "All day long at work I'm anxious and worried."* No shitty job, or person, ever makes you experience negative feelings. It's always you who are experiencing them; and then placing the blame on others. Essentially, you are emotionally pinching yourself and not letting go. People go their entire lives without releasing the pinch. Instead of letting go, they scream at others, *"Release the pain! Let go! Fix this! Stop this! You're to blame!"* Wake up and see that you are solely responsible for letting go of the pain, and you can do it now.

*15 minutes of silence and focused breathing. Repeat the mantra: *"I can release negative feelings, here and now."*

Day 28
(Share this experience using #30DaysLaugh)

Exercise:

Make yourself laugh for 5 minutes. Don't stop laughing. You might feel strange, weird, embarrassed, or stupid...it doesn't matter, just laugh. Try to laugh alone and without the aid of a comedy or joke. If you don't know how to start, just start making the noises that typically accompany your laughter.

What feelings did you experience during this exercise? Many people report feeling embarrassed or goofy, which is great; however, most people also report a feeling of relief and buoyancy when they've completed this exercise.

Similar to holding a smile, laughing for 5 minutes is a fantastic way to come into present awareness. If you think about it, humor is necessary for life. How sad is the person who is unable to laugh at the experiences of life? After all, life is funny, even the dreadful and lousy experiences.

If you ever again experience adverse thoughts and feelings about your shitty job, simply laugh at them. Consider how crazy and frivolous the shitty job and your reactions to it are; it really is a funny dependency. No other living thing on the planet becomes dependent on work that it hates. The entire situation is comical. If you perceive the shitty job for what it truly is - a fictitious, impractical, and frivolous dependency – then it can be easily dropped. You must learn to laugh at it. Genuinely laugh the shitty job away.

*15 minutes of silence and focused breathing. Repeat the mantra: **"Life is wonderful, funny, and real."**

Day 29

(Share this experience using #30DaysStack)

Exercise:

Using objects that can stack (rocks, books, boxes, containers, pillows, etc), stack them slowly and carefully until they fall.

When the stack collapses, smile and laugh.

The lives of many people are spent stacking things for the goal of success, as defined by society. People stack possessions, knowledge, relationships, degrees, money, jobs, toys, businesses, experiences, etc. They stress, fight, fatigue, compete, become ill, and get anxious and depressed through the process of stacking; yet, few people have found happiness. Society tells us that if our stack is high and mighty, we'll have obtained success. What a deception. What are you stacking; or what do you feel compelled to stack? How is your shitty job supporting that stack?

Allow the stack to fall. This lesson is not encouraging laziness; but instead teaches that real, authentic, and fulfilling work and action can only happen apart from the stress and worry of stacking. When you stack, you're focused on the future and the perceived importance of the stack; and then you have to maintain that heap of nonsense, which requires a lot of anxiety and pressure. Focus on your experience in the present moment; and if the stack falls, then smile and laugh.

*15 minutes of silence and focused breathing. Repeat the mantra: *"I allow the stack to fall."*

Day 30
(Share this experience using #30DaysThanks)

Exercise:

Take a piece of paper (one that you can keep) and write down all that you are grateful for – these things don't have to be in any particular order of importance.

Next to each thing you list, write "Thank you."

The person who isn't thankful for all that life gives is typically quite miserable; and shitty jobs thrive on that misery. The truly grateful person can let go of anything at anytime. A thankful person is always a happy person, so practice gratitude daily.

Have you ever heard anyone say, "*I'm so grateful for my shitty job*"? Nobody is thankful for shitty jobs; which is a clear sign that it's a destructive dependency. However, a few people in shitty jobs have learned to be thankful for the present moment experience.

Not only is it unhealthy, but the dependency on a shitty job discourages a grateful mind and soul. With only one life to live in the present moment, it's important to always emphasize a grateful heart. Spend time with people who are grateful, and do things that nourish a thankful heart in the present moment. Anything that encourages misery and depression isn't worth giving attention to. Be thankful, always.

*15 minutes of silence and focused breathing. Repeat the mantra: "*I am grateful. I am thankful.*"

Conclusion

By now you have learned that your shitty job is not the cause of negative thoughts and feelings. Hopefully you've been able to accept that the shittiness of your job is illusory and can be dropped at any moment. You may even have dropped your shitty perception of the job, quit, or have simply and naturally let the job go by this point. If you have not; it is advised that you repeat the exercises and lessons that were most beneficial to you.

The exercises and lessons in this program taught and encouraged observation, awareness to your present moment experience, change of perception, and awakening to true happiness, which can only be found here and now. You were shown that your negative thoughts and feelings are not caused by a shitty job, or any unhealthy reliance, but are solely within you and illusory; which means that you are capable of letting those thoughts and feelings pass and dropping the adversity. As mentioned at the beginning, there were no goals or measures of success for this program. If you were hoping to find a reason to quit a shitty job, then you may be spending too much time struggling and thinking about it.

Life is not meant to be spent asleep in a shitty job, or any toxic dependency. Wake up to the present moment and enjoy your present experience. If you've made it through the program, you are certainly more awakened then when you started; however, don't give up mindfully practicing observation of thoughts and feelings, stillness, silence, deep and focused breathing, allowing everything to pass, laughing, smiling, and being grateful. Live wonderfully awakened and aware…with or without a shitty job.

Notes for Day 1

(Use this page to write down thoughts, reminders, ideas, prayers, mantras, revelations, lessons, modifications to the exercise, or experiences. If you'd like to share something, please post using **#30DaysNow** or use the exercise's unique hashtag.)

Notes for Day 2

(Use this page to write down thoughts, reminders, ideas, prayers, mantras, revelations, lessons, modifications to the exercise, or experiences. If you'd like to share something, please post using **#30DaysNow** or use the exercise's unique hashtag.)

Notes for Day 3

(Use this page to write down thoughts, reminders, ideas, prayers, mantras, revelations, lessons, modifications to the exercise, or experiences. If you'd like to share something, please post using **#30DaysNow** or use the exercise's unique hashtag.)

Notes for Day 4

(Use this page to write down thoughts, reminders, ideas, prayers, mantras, revelations, lessons, modifications to the exercise, or experiences. If you'd like to share something, please post using **#30DaysNow** or use the exercise's unique hashtag.)

Notes for Day 5

(Use this page to write down thoughts, reminders, ideas, prayers, mantras, revelations, lessons, modifications to the exercise, or experiences. If you'd like to share something, please post using **#30DaysNow** or use the exercise's unique hashtag.)

Notes for Day 6
(Use this page to write down thoughts, reminders, ideas, prayers, mantras, revelations, lessons, modifications to the exercise, or experiences. If you'd like to share something, please post using **#30DaysNow** or use the exercise's unique hashtag.)

Notes for Day 7

(Use this page to write down thoughts, reminders, ideas, prayers, mantras, revelations, lessons, modifications to the exercise, or experiences. If you'd like to share something, please post using **#30DaysNow** or use the exercise's unique hashtag.)

Notes for Day 8
(Use this page to write down thoughts, reminders, ideas, prayers, mantras, revelations, lessons, modifications to the exercise, or experiences. If you'd like to share something, please post using **#30DaysNow** or use the exercise's unique hashtag.)

Notes for Day 9
(Use this page to write down thoughts, reminders, ideas, prayers, mantras, revelations, lessons, modifications to the exercise, or experiences. If you'd like to share something, please post using **#30DaysNow** or use the exercise's unique hashtag.)

Notes for Day 10

(Use this page to write down thoughts, reminders, ideas, prayers, mantras, revelations, lessons, modifications to the exercise, or experiences. If you'd like to share something, please post using **#30DaysNow** or use the exercise's unique hashtag.)

Notes for Day 11
(Use this page to write down thoughts, reminders, ideas, prayers, mantras, revelations, lessons, modifications to the exercise, or experiences. If you'd like to share something, please post using **#30DaysNow** or use the exercise's unique hashtag.)

Notes for Day 12

(Use this page to write down thoughts, reminders, ideas, prayers, mantras, revelations, lessons, modifications to the exercise, or experiences. If you'd like to share something, please post using **#30DaysNow** or use the exercise's unique hashtag.)

Notes for Day 13

(Use this page to write down thoughts, reminders, ideas, prayers, mantras, revelations, lessons, modifications to the exercise, or experiences. If you'd like to share something, please post using **#30DaysNow** or use the exercise's unique hashtag.)

Notes for Day 14
(Use this page to write down thoughts, reminders, ideas, prayers, mantras, revelations, lessons, modifications to the exercise, or experiences. If you'd like to share something, please post using **#30DaysNow** or use the exercise's unique hashtag.)

Notes for Day 15
(Use this page to write down thoughts, reminders, ideas, prayers, mantras, revelations, lessons, modifications to the exercise, or experiences. If you'd like to share something, please post using **#30DaysNow** or use the exercise's unique hashtag.)

Notes for Day 16

(Use this page to write down thoughts, reminders, ideas, prayers, mantras, revelations, lessons, modifications to the exercise, or experiences. If you'd like to share something, please post using **#30DaysNow** or use the exercise's unique hashtag.)

Notes for Day 17

(Use this page to write down thoughts, reminders, ideas, prayers, mantras, revelations, lessons, modifications to the exercise, or experiences. If you'd like to share something, please post using **#30DaysNow** or use the exercise's unique hashtag.)

Notes for Day 18

(Use this page to write down thoughts, reminders, ideas, prayers, mantras, revelations, lessons, modifications to the exercise, or experiences. If you'd like to share something, please post using **#30DaysNow** or use the exercise's unique hashtag.)

Notes for Day 19

(Use this page to write down thoughts, reminders, ideas, prayers, mantras, revelations, lessons, modifications to the exercise, or experiences. If you'd like to share something, please post using **#30DaysNow** or use the exercise's unique hashtag.)

Notes for Day 20
(Use this page to write down thoughts, reminders, ideas, prayers, mantras, revelations, lessons, modifications to the exercise, or experiences. If you'd like to share something, please post using **#30DaysNow** or use the exercise's unique hashtag.)

Notes for Day 21
(Use this page to write down thoughts, reminders, ideas, prayers, mantras, revelations, lessons, modifications to the exercise, or experiences. If you'd like to share something, please post using **#30DaysNow** or use the exercise's unique hashtag.)

Notes for Day 22

(Use this page to write down thoughts, reminders, ideas, prayers, mantras, revelations, lessons, modifications to the exercise, or experiences. If you'd like to share something, please post using **#30DaysNow** or use the exercise's unique hashtag.)

Notes for Day 23

(Use this page to write down thoughts, reminders, ideas, prayers, mantras, revelations, lessons, modifications to the exercise, or experiences. If you'd like to share something, please post using **#30DaysNow** or use the exercise's unique hashtag.)

Notes for Day 24
(Use this page to write down thoughts, reminders, ideas, prayers, mantras, revelations, lessons, modifications to the exercise, or experiences. If you'd like to share something, please post using **#30DaysNow** or use the exercise's unique hashtag.)

Notes for Day 25

(Use this page to write down thoughts, reminders, ideas, prayers, mantras, revelations, lessons, modifications to the exercise, or experiences. If you'd like to share something, please post using **#30DaysNow** or use the exercise's unique hashtag.)

Notes for Day 26

(Use this page to write down thoughts, reminders, ideas, prayers, mantras, revelations, lessons, modifications to the exercise, or experiences. If you'd like to share online, please post using **#30DaysNow** or use the exercise's unique hashtag.)

Notes for Day 27
(Use this page to write down thoughts, reminders, ideas, prayers, mantras, revelations, lessons, modifications to the exercise, or experiences. If you'd like to share something, please post using **#30DaysNow** or use the exercise's unique hashtag.)

Notes for Day 28

(Use this page to write down thoughts, reminders, ideas, prayers, mantras, revelations, lessons, modifications to the exercise, or experiences. If you'd like to share something, please post using **#30DaysNow** or use the exercise's unique hashtag.)

Notes for Day 29

(Use this page to write down thoughts, reminders, ideas, prayers, mantras, revelations, lessons, modifications to the exercise, or experiences. If you'd like to share something, please post using **#30DaysNow** or use the exercise's unique hashtag.)

Notes for Day 30

(Use this page to write down thoughts, reminders, ideas, prayers, mantras, revelations, lessons, modifications to the exercise, or experiences. If you'd like to share something, please post using **#30DaysNow** or use the exercise's unique hashtag.)

To be mindful is to experience life in the present moment...it's the only moment we have.

Don't forget to leave an online review.

Thank you!

www.ingramcontent.com/pod-product-compliance
Lightning Source LLC
Chambersburg PA
CBHW022109170526
45157CB00004B/1547